On the Paranormal Hunt

SEARCHING for BERMUDA TRIANGLE ANSWERS

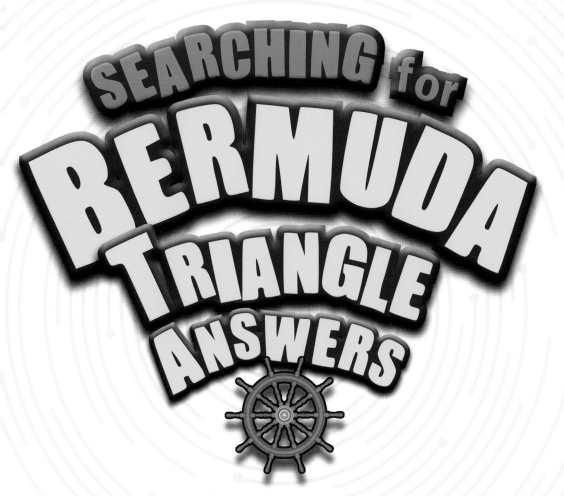

Thomas Kingsley Troupe

BLACK
RABBIT
BOOKS

Hi Jinx is published by Black Rabbit Books
P.O. Box 3263, Mankato, Minnesota, 56002.
www.blackrabbitbooks.com
Copyright © 2021 Black Rabbit Books

Marysa Storm, editor; Grant Gould & Michael
Sellner, designers; Omay Ayres, photo researcher

Cataloging-in-Publication Data is available at the Library of Congress.
ISBN 978-1-62310-315-6 (library binding)
ISBN 978-1-64466-411-7 (paperback)
ISBN 978-1-62310-409-2 (e-book)

Printed in the United States. 1/20

Image Credits

Alamy: AF archive, 4–5; PJF Military Collection, 16; Science Photo Library, Cover;
Sven Bachström, 16; coastguard.dodlive.mil: Petty Officer 3rd Class Bob Gross/U.S.
Coast Guard, 8–9; iStock: guvendemir, 18–19;
Shutterstock: aapsky, 11; Algol, 12; Anton Balazh,
6–7; Artsem Vysotski, Back Cover, 1, 11, 21; Big Boy,
2–3, 19; Denis Cristo, 21; designer_an, 8;
Dreamcreation, 3, 18; ekler, 9; Elena100, Cover, 1,
22; m.mphoto, 20; Pasko Maksim, Back Cover,
17, 23, 24; penang, 11; picoStudio, 13, 14–15,
18; Pitju, 10, 21; Ron Dale, 5, 9, 13, 20;
Rvector, 5; S.Bachstroem, 11; Skycolors,
14–15; tsuneomp, 3
Every effort has been made to contact copyright
holders for material reproduced in this book. Any
omissions will be rectified in subsequent printings
if notice is given to the publisher.

CONTENTS

Chapter 1

LOST AT SEA

Waves crash against a ship. The boat rocks as water splashes across the deck. The captain and crew are all shouting. The radio and **compasses** aren't working. Lightning flashes. Thunder roars.

There's a sudden bright light. And just like that, the boat is gone. It seems to have disappeared. Did the Bermuda Triangle strike again?

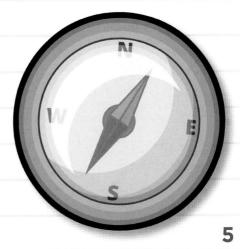

A Strange Spot

People tell stories about weird things happening in the Bermuda Triangle. The Bermuda Triangle is an area in the Atlantic Ocean. It stretches from Miami to Puerto Rico to Bermuda. People say planes and ships disappear while traveling through it. The planes and ships are never seen again.

Experts study the spot for clues. They want to know if something strange is really going on.

Miami

Bermuda

BERMUDA TRIANGLE

Puerto Rico

Chapter 2

RESEARCHERS

People have studied the Triangle. They want to know what causes disappearances. Researchers work with **oceanographers** and other scientists. These experts study the Triangle's water movement and weather. They wonder if big storms could be the answer. Researchers also work with the U.S. Coast Guard. When people go missing, the Guard looks for them.

Not everyone agrees on the Triangle's size. This disagreement makes the area hard to study.

Tools of the Trade

People need special tools to study the ocean. They use **satellites** to track storms. Underwater robots help them search for **wreckage**. Investigators also interview people. They take notes. They research stories to make sure they're true.

satellite

underwater robot

Chapter 3

INVESTIGATE!

For years, people have researched the Triangle. Journalist Larry Kusche studied stories that took place between 1840 and 1973. Kusche realized many stories were completely made-up. Others had been poorly reported. They were missing information. Often, storms caused ships to crash and sink. They didn't disappear.

Ships often travel through the Triangle without problems.

Poorly Prepared

The cases the U.S. Coast Guard investigated weren't disappearances, either. The boats or planes went off course or crashed. In 2016, the Guard said the reason for most accidents was pilot **error**. About 82 percent of reported accidents involved poorly trained people. These people didn't bring the right tools. They got lost easily. When bad luck or weather struck, they didn't know what to do.

Some people think sea monsters live in the Triangle. So far, none have been found.

USS *Cyclops*

Giant Waves

Some large ships have gone missing in the Triangle. People wonder how. Some scientists think **rogue** waves are the answer. These huge waves happen suddenly. There's no time to call for help.

Scientists researched the idea. They built a model of the USS *Cyclops*. It was a ship that disappeared in the area. They then tested the model in a **simulator**. The tests showed a rogue wave could break the ship in two. It would have sunk in minutes.

The USS *Cyclops* went missing in 1918. More than 300 people disappeared with it.

Where's the Proof?

Is something strange really happening? Most people don't think so. Many stories are made-up. And other events often have normal explanations. Still, some disappearances haven't been solved. Maybe something strange really is going on!

Chapter 4

GET in on the HI JINX

The truth about the Bermuda Triangle could still be out there. And you can be part of the hunt. Study pictures of the Triangle. Read stories about disappearances. The Atlantic Ocean is huge. People still don't know all of its secrets. Maybe someday you'll discover them!

Take It One Step More

1. Would you travel through the Triangle? Why or why not?

2. **Many Triangle stories aren't true. People made parts up. Why do you think people do that?**

3. What do you think happened to people who disappeared in the Triangle?

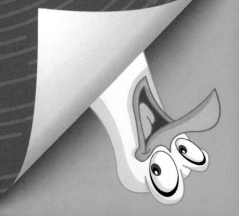

GLOSSARY

compass (KUM-pus)—a tool used to find direction

error (ER-er)—a wrong action or statement

oceanographer (oh-shuh-NOG-ruh-fuhr)—a scientist who deals with the ocean

rogue (ROHG)—someone or something that is different from others usually in a dangerous or harmful way

satellite (SA-tuh-liyt)—a machine sent into space that moves around the earth, moon, sun, or other planet

simulator (SIM-yuh-lay-tuhr)—a device that lets the user practice under test conditions

wreckage (RE-kij)—broken and disordered parts from something destroyed

BOOKS

Bowman, Chris. *Flight 19: Lost in the Bermuda Triangle.* Paranormal Mysteries. Minneapolis: Bellwether Media, Inc., 2020.

Loh-Hagan, Virginia. *Bermuda Triangle.* Urban Legends: Don't Read Alone! Ann Arbor, MI: Cherry Lake Publishing, 2018.

Richard, Orlin. *Investigating the Bermuda Triangle.* World's Greatest Mysteries. New York: AV2 by Weigl, 2020.

WEBSITES

Bermuda Triangle – Kids
kids.britannica.com/kids/article/Bermuda-Triangle/598956

Bermuda Triangle Mystery
www.sciencekids.co.nz/sciencefacts/earth/bermudatriangle.html

What Is the Bermuda Triangle?
oceanservice.noaa.gov/facts/bermudatri.html

INDEX